Should Billy Brush His Teeth?

Taking Care of Yourself

Rebecca Rissman

Raintree is an imprint of Capstone Global Library Limited, a company incorporated in England and Wales having its registered office at 7 Pilgrim Street, London, EC4V 6LB – Registered company number: 6695582

www.raintreepublishers.co.uk
myorders@raintreepublishers.co.uk

Text © Capstone Global Library Limited 2013
First published in hardback in 2013
First published in paperback in 2014
The moral rights of the proprietor have been asserted.

Edited by Daniel Nunn, Rebecca Rissman, and Siân Smith
Designed by Steve Mead
Picture research by Mica Brancic
Production by Alison Parsons
Originated by Capstone Global Library Ltd
Printed and bound in China

ISBN 978 1 406 25330 6 (hardback)
16 15 14 13 12
10 9 8 7 6 5 4 3 2 1

ISBN 978 1 406 25337 5 (paperback)
17 16 15 14 13
10 9 8 7 6 5 4 3 2 1

British Library Cataloguing in Publication Data
Rissman, Rebecca.
  Should Billy brush his teeth?. -- (What would you do?)
  1. Teeth--Care and hygiene--Juvenile literature.
  I. Title II. Series
  613.4-dc23

Acknowledgements
All photographs © Capstone Publishers (Karon Dubke).

Every effort has been made to contact copyright holders of material reproduced in this book. Any omissions will be rectified in subsequent printings if notice is given to the publisher.

Contents

Making choices

We make choices every day, such as "Should I mop up my drink?"

Our choices have effects.

Ask yourself if your choices will have good or bad effects.

Should Billy brush his teeth?

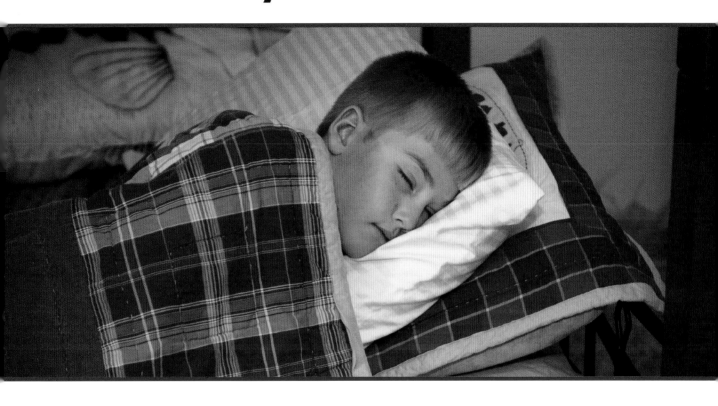

Every night, Billy goes to bed. Should Billy brush his teeth first?

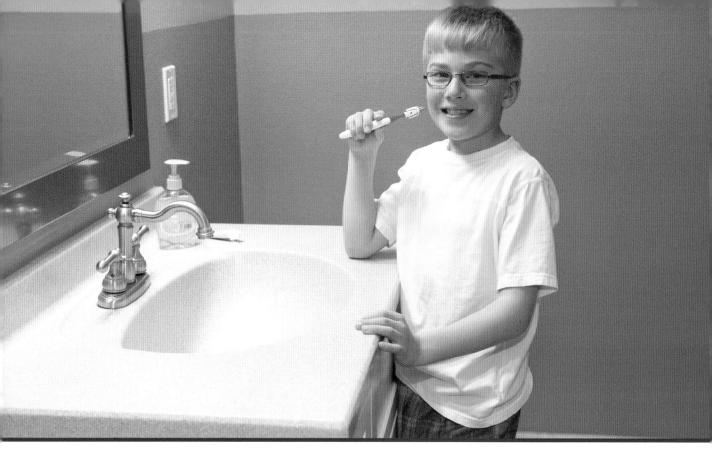

Billy could choose to brush his teeth
every night.

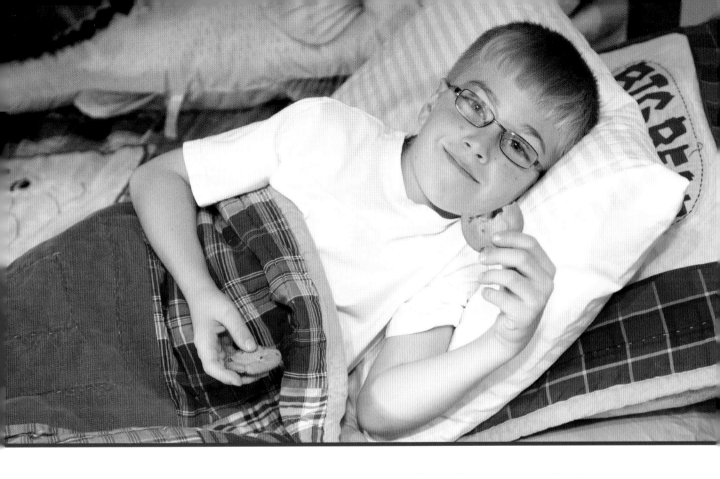

Billy could choose not to brush his teeth every night.

What would YOU have done?

If Billy had brushed his teeth every night, they would have stayed clean and healthy. If Billy had not brushed his teeth, they could have gone bad and become painful.

Should Charlotte wear suncream?

It is a sunny day. Should Charlotte wear suncream?

Charlotte could choose to wear suncream.

Charlotte could choose not to wear suncream.

What would YOU have done?

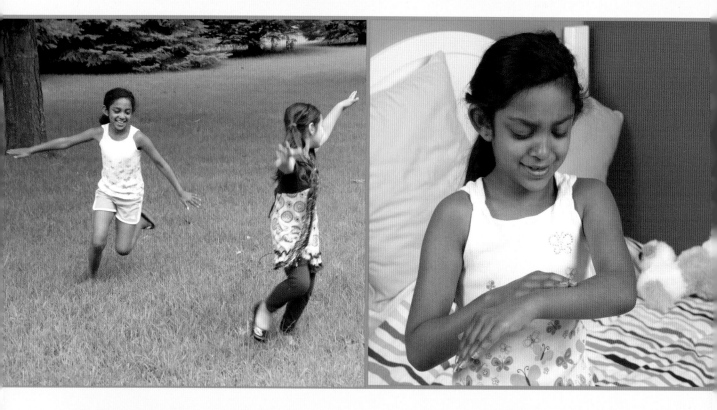

If Charlotte had worn suncream, her skin would have stayed healthy in the sun. If she had not worn suncream, she might have burnt her skin in the sun.

Should Theo have a shower?

Theo is dirty from playing outside.
Should Theo have a shower?

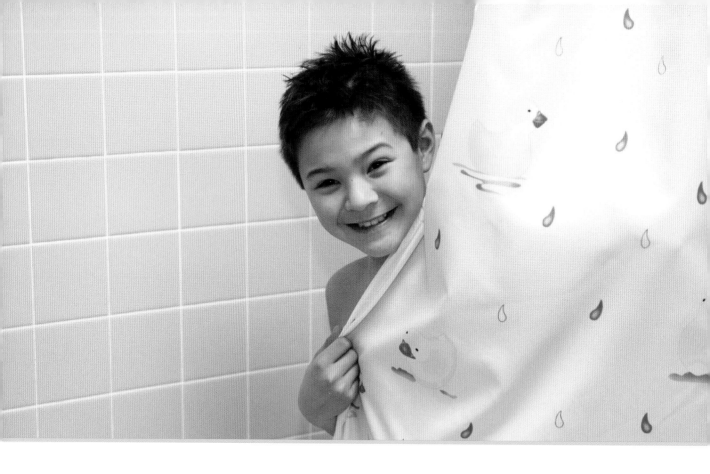

Theo could choose to have a shower.

Theo could choose not to have
a shower.

What would YOU have done?

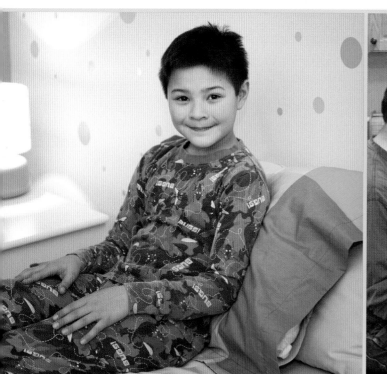 

If Theo had taken a shower, he would have kept his body and hair clean and healthy. If he had not had a shower, he might have started to smell, or even made himself ill.

Should Wendy wear clean clothes?

It is time for school. Should Wendy wear clean clothes?

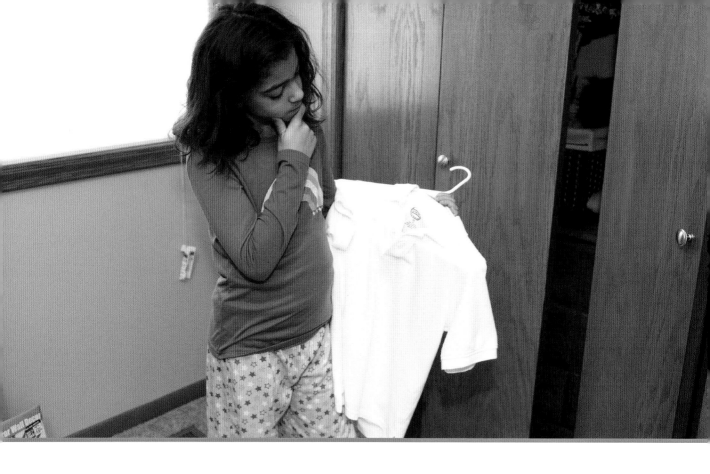

Wendy could choose to wear clean clothes.

Wendy could choose to wear dirty clothes.

What would YOU have done?

If Wendy had not worn clean clothes, her clothes might not have smelled nice, and her friends might not have wanted to sit beside her. If she had worn clean clothes to school, she would have looked smart and smelled nice.

Picture glossary

choice a decision

effects the results of a decision or something you choose to do. Choices can have good or bad effects.

healthy fit and well

suncream special cream you use to keep your skin safe in the sun

Index

Notes for parents and teachers

Before reading

Explain to children that there are consequences, or outcomes, for each of their decisions. List a few examples from their daily routine. For example, *if you decide not to eat your lunch, you might feel hungry later; if you decide to wait your turn at the water fountain, everyone will get a chance to drink.* Ask children to come up with their own examples of decisions and consequences.

After reading

Turn to page 7. Explain to the children that Billy must decide whether or not to brush his teeth before he goes to sleep. Show children the photos on page 10 and explain that each shows a different outcome. Ask children which seems better. Encourage children to discuss why they think brushing their teeth is important.